"The King in Me"

A practical guide designed to help men of color discover their life's purpose through self-exploration, healing, and personal development.

Dr. Solomon Tention

The King in Me

Copyright © 2020 by SIM EDU Consulting, LLC

Printed in the United States of America

https://simeduconsulting.com/

Dedication

I dedicate this book to my amazing family who have always been my biggest source of inspiration. My family has not only been a consistent support system but also have served as accountability partners and mentors as I have progressed through the various highs and lows of life. Without their love and support, I would not be the man that I am today.

I dedicate this book to my best friends who continuously remind me of the importance of strong men within your community. These men proudly serve as my mentors, and routinely demonstrate to me the standard of manhood in the capacity of leaders for their homes, husbands to the wives, and fathers to their children.

I dedicate this book to each of my academic and professional mentors who have left positive impressions in my life.

I dedicate this book to the hundreds of students within both the secondary, undergraduate, and graduate levels whom I have been blessed to serve.

I dedicate this book to men of color around the world in their struggle to discover and master their life's purpose and assignment.

I dedicate this book to God – the ultimate creator of men.

Table of Contents

About the Author

Dr. Solomon Tention is as a higher education administrator, professor, and entrepreneur serving as the CEO of SIM Companies. As a student success scholar, and student affairs administrator, Solomon has authored several articles, book chapters, and publications. He has also conducted several presentations at various universities and national conferences. Solomon also serves on the Review Board for the Journal of Underrepresented and Minority Progress. He maintains a research agenda that focuses on Student Affairs, Cultural Competency, Diversity & Inclusion, Social Capital, Educational Psychology, Internationalization, Social Justice, Community Colleges, and Student Success. Solomon has earned a Bachelor's Degree in Sociology, a Master's Degree in Education in Teaching & Learning with a specialization in General Education Instruction, Leadership, and a Doctorate Degree of Education with a specialization in Higher Education Leadership.

Welcome

Welcome my brother and my friend. Thank you for purchasing this guide and self-development journal designed for men of color who wish to embark on their personal journeys of "purpose discovery."

As I write this forward, one of the hardest lessons that I have learned throughout my life's journey is that, as humans, we all crave purpose and meaning more than survival. Without a clear purpose, men find themselves engaging in "purpose deterring" activities, relationships, and experiences. We find ourselves always living in "survival" mode, or on a "hamster wheel," like mentality, never experiencing the fullness of life that we were intended to have.

Before you begin your journey by progressing through this guide and self-development journal, I want to present you with the disclaimer that "purpose discovery" is hard work! If done right, you may find yourself in deep personal reflection, displaying a range of unexpected emotions, reliving painful experiences or situations, etc. You must be willing to do the deep "inner" work of self-reflection and healing if you want to seriously embrace the purpose discovery process.

Your purpose is not some idea that you have to "create" or "find," hence why this journey focuses on "discovery." When you were born, you were given everything you needed to executive your life's purpose and assignment. As you begin this process and start doubting your skills, remember that everything you have is all you need. How are men blinded from purpose? Some of the many examples include, life's various challenges and experiences, such as our environment, relationships, and unaddressed developmental or other forms of severe trauma.

Your purpose is also not a "single" thing. It is your life's overall assignment that can be fulfilled as you grow through various capacities. As you grow how you live out your assignment may change but your assignment itself will remain consistent. I don't want you want to begin this journey with the belief that this book is focused on helping you find a career, i.e., doctor, lawyer, musician, welder, etc.? We will discuss this further as you dive into this resource.

I am hopeful that each of you will embrace some of the contents within this resource to take control of your life, discover your purpose, and begin to write your story.

Sincerely,

Dr. Solomon Tention
CEO & Founder
SIM Companies
stention@simeduconsulting.com
@_simcompanies
@dr.solomontention

SECTION **1**

How to Use this Six-Step Guide & Journal?

I was very intentional in not creating a day-by-day journal because I understand that for some of you, this may take either weeks or even months. I do not want you to feel stressed about meeting goals or milestones in this resource; my ultimate desire is to provide you with the tools to begin TODAY! This guide and journal are organized into sections to include, Section (1) - How to Use this Guide, Section (2) - 6 Step Guide to Discovering Your Purpose, Section (3) - Beginning your Discovery Process, Section (4) - Living A Life On Purpose and Section (5) - Living a Life of Purpose: Ongoing Support.

Below are some of my recommendations to get the most out of this process:

- Identify and create a safe and quiet environment for reading, writing, and reflection.
- Pray each day before you begin your discovery process. (See Purpose Discovery Prayer Below)
- Identify the best day and time to engage in journal activities.
- Be consistent.
- If you miss a day, make plans to do it the day after.
- Do not place added pressure on yourself to do more than one activity per day.
- You may get frustrated, stop, reflect, and make places to start again.
- As you progress, stop, reflect, and remember to also read past prompts.
- Have fun, be present, and enjoy the process of self-discovery.

🙏 Purpose Discovery Prayer

Dear Father-

Thank you for this opportunity for personal reflection. As I engage in this process, please open my mind and heart to discover the purpose that you have assigned for my life. I am not perfect *(discuss your mistakes).* In addition to my mistakes, there have been circumstances in my life that I now realize have created barriers preventing me from discovering and walking in my life's purpose. However, that cycle ends today. I am committed to breaking down each of those barriers and surrendering my life to your will. I want to experience all that you have for me. I trust that you will give me grace, favor, and lead me through this process in Jesus name.

Amen

"More men fail through lack of purpose than lack of talent."
– Billy Sunday

First Read, Then Reflect, Next…How does this quote apply to my life?

_____

_____

_____

_____

_____

_____

SECTION 2

A Six-Step Guide to Discover Your Purpose

Step 1: "Unpack, Unpack, and Unpack Again"	• Take some time within this first step to take a deep dive into your life's journey. • To help organize your thoughts, create a timeline (see below) or use notepads to discuss your experiences in chronological order. (The good, bad, ugly, and accomplishments) • At some point during this process, you may need the support of a therapist, community group, pastor, or a mentor to help process your experiences there are some connections to various forms trauma.
Step 2: "Sense-Making"	• Have you allowed your experiences to create mental prisons for you? Have you given more power to your trauma than you should have? • Research indicates that sense-making is the process by which people give meaning to their collective experiences. It has been defined as "the ongoing retrospective development of plausible images that rationalize what people are doing" (Weick, Sutcliffe, & Obstfeld, 2005, p. 409). During this stage, take

	some time to list key watershed moments within your experiences and use the activity within this guide to engage in the foundational stages of the sense-making process.
Step 3: "Why did I survive?"	• It is important to not just acknowledge that you survived, but to also ask yourself, "why did I survive? How could those experiences be viewed differently? I have found that there is a distinct difference between living as a "victim" and "victimhood." • We are all victims of something, i.e our past traumas, environmental circumstances, etc. • The goal is to do the deep inner work to ensure that we never enter into within the state of victimhood – it becomes our "state of mind." This mindset presents a barrier to discover your life's purpose.
Step 4: "What is my purpose?	• During this stage, you will seek to answer the critical question of what did the creator have in mind when you were placed on the earth. How can your life serve as his messenger? • The creator gives us our purpose first, and other factors may determine our vocation. • Within this guide you will find activities that strategically challenge you through various phases of purpose discovery.
Step 5: Setting Goals	• During this stage, you discover some of the foundational elements centered on your life's purpose. To be "lived," setting

	goals will be necessary.
	• Goals provide you with focus, measures progress, and keep you undistracted to any activity or relationship that is not aligned with your purpose.
Step 6: Building Relationships	• During this stage, you should examine your relationships to ensure alignment with your purpose. Who in your life holds you accountable? Have you chosen the right source who can help you fulfill your life's "purpose" spouse? Who your mentors who share the same purpose? Do I have the right *team* around me that will support and cultivate my purpose?
	• A few years ago, my work was highlighted in a book chapter that chronicled the stories of African American scholars. In that book I talked about the importance of bonds, bridges, and linkages throughout my academic success. Within this guide, you will find some experiences to help you begin to identify and define these types of relationships.

"Healing begins where the wound was made."
–Alice Walker

First Read, Then Reflect, Next...How does this quote apply to my life?

_____

_____

_____

_____

_____

_____

✏️ Reflecting on Your Life Timeline

Instructions: Think about the effective events that you have experienced throughout your life. Please, be sure to place them in order on this chart. When you are finished, answer the reflection question below.

Early Childhood	Elementary School	Middle School	High School	Post-High School	Adult Life

Reflection: What did you discover about yourself and characteristics that are important to you?

_____

_____

_____

_____

_____

_____

_____

_____

_____

_____

"Sense-Making" Activity

What are some of the triggers from some of your life's past experiences?

_____

_____

_____

_____

_____

_____

How did those triggers make you feel or what emotions present themselves?

_____

_____

_____

_____

_____

_____

What are some of the external factors that contributed to these experiences?

_____

_____

_____

_____

_____

_____

How did those experiences affect me?

_____
_____
_____
_____
_____
_____

What did I learn?

_____
_____
_____
_____
_____
_____

Why did I survive?

_____
_____
_____
_____
_____
_____

Sense-Making Activity Reflection

SECTION 3

Beginning Your Discovery Process

Author's Note: "Thought Leaders" are individuals or firms who are influential in a specific subject matter. As you progress through this journey, I would like you to take some time to research each of these African American thought leaders. I have personally studied some of them throughout my purpose discovery journey. You can find them on various platforms where they routinely provide content that is focused on the power of *purpose*. Just type in their name in your search engine along with "purpose," and you will gain access to various types of content that you should plan to read and build into your weekly personal-development time. I would also recommend that you utilize YouTube as your "university". There you will find thousands of lectures, discussions, sermons, etc. from each of these thought leaders around purpose discovery. You will also find various personal stories of individuals who have also engaged in purpose discovery work. You may also find connection, strength, and encouragement from their discovery journeys.

Purpose Discovery Focused Thought Leaders

Tony Dungy
Dr. Myles Monroe
Reginald Foreman
Wes Moore
Russell Simmons
Bishop TD Jakes
Pastor Toure Roberts
Zachary Rinkins
Dr. Anita Philips
Dr. Dharius Daniel
Calvin Mills, Jr.
Pastor Jerry Flowers
Kenneth Braswell

📝 Journal Entry

What are the two moments that you will never forget in your life? What makes them so memorable?

_____

_____

_____

_____

_____

_____

_____

_____

_____

_____

_____

_____

_____

_____

_____

_____

_____

_____

_____

_____

_____

_____

_____

"If you can't figure out your purpose, figure out your passion. For your passion will lead you right into your purpose."
–TD Jakes

First Read, Then Reflect, Next...How does this quote apply to my life?

_____

_____

_____

_____

Journal Entry

What are some questions that you urgently need answers to? (Author's Note: Stop here to seek some answers to these questions. Do not allow it to overwhelm you and stop your process. You may never find the answers, but engaging in this process is the start to your personal freedom.)

_____
_____
_____
_____
_____
_____
_____
_____
_____
_____
_____
_____
_____
_____
_____
_____
_____
_____
_____
_____
_____
_____
_____
_____
_____
_____

Forgiveness Exercise

Who have I been holding a grudge against?	What was the offense?	How did the offense make me feel?	Have I allowed bitterness toward this person to consume my thoughts? (Yes or No)	I chose to forgive _____ (person name) on _____(date).... (MM/DD/YR)

Forgiveness Reflection

"Unfortunately, many of us often spend our lives doing what we were trained to do. Some do what they were asked to do. And most of us do what others need us to do. And all the while, we wonder why the feeling of fulfillment eludes us."
- TD Jakes

First Read, Then Reflect, Next…How does this quote apply to my life?

_____

_____

_____

_____

✏️ Journal Entry

If I could talk to my teenage self, what would I say?

_____

_____

_____

_____

_____

_____

_____

_____

_____

_____

_____

_____

_____

_____

_____

_____

_____

_____

_____

_____

_____

_____

_____

*A life is not important
except in the impact it has
on other lives.
– Jackie Robinson*

**First Read, Then Reflect, Next…How
does this quote apply to my life?**

_____

_____

_____

_____

_____

_____

_____

📔 Journal Entry

What are some of my takeaways from life's biggest mistakes?

_____
_____
_____
_____
_____
_____
_____
_____
_____
_____
_____
_____
_____
_____
_____
_____
_____
_____
_____
_____
_____
_____
_____
_____

✎📖 Journal Entry

You are a man but you are also HUMAN. There are going to be some past experiences that irritate you and you can't seem to forget. It may be a negative experience or interaction with someone or past mistakes. Write them down, pray, and give YOURSELF GRACE. Let it go!

_____

_____

_____

_____

_____

_____

_____

_____

_____

_____

_____

_____

_____

_____

_____

_____

_____

_____

_____

_____

Journal Entry

What do I want to get out of my life? What actions steps should I take to experience the life I desire?

_____

_____

_____

_____

_____

_____

_____

_____

_____

_____

_____

_____

_____

_____

_____

_____

_____

_____

_____

_____

_____

_____

_____

"The cave you fear to enter holds the treasure you seek"
-Joseph Campbell

First Read, Then Reflect, Next...How does this quote apply to my life?

_____

_____

_____

_____

_____

_____

_____

✏️ Journal Entry

I would like more _____ in my life and why.

_____

_____

_____

_____

_____

_____

_____

_____

_____

_____

_____

_____

_____

_____

_____

_____

_____

_____

_____

_____

_____

_____

_____

_____

_____

_____

👑 Projection & Labels

What is projection? Psychological projection is a defense mechanism people subconsciously employ to cope with difficult feelings or emotions. Psychological projection involves projecting undesirable feelings or emotions onto someone else, rather than admitting to or dealing with unwanted feelings. (Everyday Health.Com)

What negative labels or projections or insecurities have you allowed your past and others to "project" on to you and your CROWN?

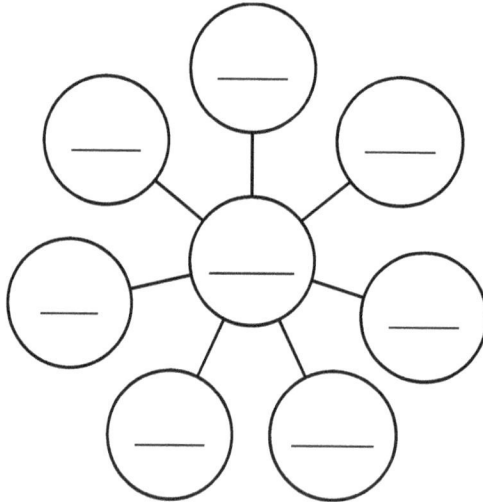

Projection Activity Reflection

_____

_____

_____

_____

_____

_____

_____

Value Clarification

Instructions: Circle the values that are most important to you. After reviewing the list, put a star by your top ten values.

Values: Adventure, Beauty, Balance, Challenge, Community, Fun, Harmony, Personal, Growth, Relationships, Spiritual, Fulfillment, Stability, Freedom, Competence, Social Justice, Achievement, Collaboration, Creativity, Cultural Heritage, Curiosity, Equity, Fairness, Family, Friendship, Hard Work, Honesty, making a Difference, Humor, Integrity, Health, Independence, Intelligence, Learning, Love, Openness, Power, Quiet, Responsibility, Teamwork, Trust, Wealth, Belonging, Authenticity

Are there any other values important to you that are not listed here?

_____

_____

_____

_____

_____

_____

_____

_____

_____

_____

If you had to narrow your list down to your top five values, what would it be?

_____

_____

_____

_____

_____

_____

_____

_____

_____

_____

_____

✏️ Journal Entry

What are the top 10 things that bring you the most joy?

_____

_____

_____

_____

_____

_____

_____

_____

_____

_____

_____

_____

_____

_____

_____

_____

_____

_____

_____

_____

_____

_____

_____

*What you're thinking is
what you're becoming.
– Muhammad Ali*

**First Read, Then Reflect, Next...How
does this quote apply to my life?**

_____

_____

_____

_____

_____

_____

_____

🎁 Self as Gift

Imagine yourself as a gift. If you are a gift to the world because of your unique personality, skills, talents . . . how would you describe the gift that you offer or the king you are?

_____
_____
_____
_____
_____
_____
_____
_____
_____

What type of effect can you (gift) have on others?

_____
_____
_____
_____
_____
_____
_____
_____
_____

Journal Entry

What do you love about life?

_____

_____

_____

_____

_____

_____

_____

_____

_____

_____

_____

_____

_____

_____

_____

_____

_____

_____

_____

_____

_____

_____

_____

"It's not enough to have lived. We should be determined to live for something."
— Winston S. Churchill

First Read, Then Reflect, Next…How does this quote apply to my life?

_____

_____

_____

_____

_____

_____

♚ The King *In* Me

What's My Personality & Style?

_____
_____
_____
_____
_____
_____
_____
_____
_____

What's does the creator say about me?

_____
_____
_____
_____
_____
_____
_____
_____
_____

What talents do I possess?

_____

_____

_____

_____

_____

_____

As a KING I am committed to:

_____

_____

_____

_____

_____

_____

Reflection

_____

_____

_____

_____

_____

_____

Journal Entry

Who do you want to be?

_____

_____

_____

_____

_____

_____

_____

_____

_____

_____

_____

_____

_____

_____

_____

_____

_____

_____

_____

_____

_____

_____

_____

_____

_____

_____

The purpose of life is a life of purpose."
– Robert Byrne

First Read, Then Reflect, Next...How does this quote apply to my life?

_____

_____

_____

_____

_____

_____

_____

Discovering Your Purpose

I believe that your *personal purpose statement* defines **who you are**. This statement reflects your passions and values. Your sense of purpose helps you gain clarity on goals and better align and define appropriate relationships. Your personal purpose statement should be between one to two sentences. Your purpose should also be aligned with your core values. Napoleon Hill, author of _definite chief aim_) created a firm foundation of success, stated, *"What a different story man would have to tell if only they would adopt a definite purpose and stand by that purpose until it had time to become an all-consuming obsession!"*

Action Steps

Brainstorm:	Allow time for quiet reflection and think about the following questions. • What did I learn about myself after completing the journal prompts within this journal? • How can I make a difference in this world? • How do I want to be remembered? • What type of legacy do I want to leave behind?
Compose Your First Draft:	Use your answers to these questions to guide your writing: • Who am I? • What do I do? • Who do I do it for? • What do they want or need? • How are they changed?
Authors Note:	• At this point of your process, it's important that you give yourself grace and permission to write your purpose statement without making corrections. • Don't over-analyze or overthink it. • Write something, reflect, and then edit it later. This process takes time, it may come overnight, or perhaps

	take a few weeks. Either way, it's OK! What is important is that you have begun to take these most important steps.
Choose Words that Reflect Positive Action:	• Instead of stating what you want to avoid, choose affirmative words and reflect on what you want to be, what you want to do, and what you would like others to experience as a result of you being on this earth.
Write in Present Tense:	• Your purpose statement is a reflection of who you are and what you intend bring to the world. Focus your target on what you envision for your life. Describe the individual mark you want to make on this planet. For Example, "I am," "I do;" not "I will".
Revise Your Statement:	• Your purpose statement is a work in progress. It will evolve over time. As you grow, you will find different avenues to serve your purpose. What is important is that you are living from this core purpose. For example, my purpose centers around building ecosystems that help individuals experience success. I live out this purpose as an administrator, business owner, author, professor, and other capacities. While I am blessed to serve in these different capacities, each one is connected to my overall purpose.
Sign It:	• Allow space for your signature at the bottom of your purpose statement. A signature reflects a commitment to your words. As a result, you will make choices that align with your purpose statement and, consequently, your goals.
Display It	• Frame or display your personal purpose statement in a place where you will see it. • The daily reminder of seeing, reading, reflecting upon, and internalizing your personal purpose statement becomes a directional compass that will guide your words, actions, decisions, and behaviors. A personal purpose statement steers your talent, determination, and commitment in a specific direction. (Source: Dr. Julie Conner, TED Speaker, Educator & Author)

Purpose Statement Draft:

Examples:

"I serve others as a visionary leader and apply ethical principles in management to make a significant difference in the world."

"My purpose is to build a bridge of understanding and be a tower of integrity to others as a speaker, writer, and entrepreneur."

I inspire the world. I help others identify their gifts and transform goals into reality."

_____

_____

_____

_____

_____

_____

Purpose Statement- Final

_____

_____

_____

_____

_____

_____

📝 Journal Entry

Reflect on your purpose?

_____

_____

_____

_____

_____

_____

_____

_____

_____

_____

_____

_____

_____

_____

_____

_____

_____

_____

_____

_____

_____

_____

_____

_____

SECTION 4:

Living a Life of Purpose

Author's Note

Congratulations! You have arrived at this section and now you would have found some joy in discovering your purpose. I want to take a moment to inform you that while you think the hard part is over, it's really just the beginning. This entire section is focused on empowering you as men of color to "live out" your everyday lives in purpose. When I reflect on this period of growth throughout my own journey, it can often be harder than the discovery process itself.

MY STORY

At this point you have discovered the foundational elements of your purpose, you may be beginning to recognize that what you have discovered was not your first choice. Surprise! If told you at the beginning of this book that you may discover that your life's purpose may not be your first choice? Or that your purpose might make you uncomfortable? You might have put this book away and sought help from another source. Many people run from purpose because they inherently have some insight on what the creator has called them to do, but because of fear they choose to not serve in purpose and experience the fullness the life. They rather be in bondage and comfortable. Eliminating our preference and comfortability are one of the methods that the creator often uses help us learn to trust him.

I never wanted to be an educator. It was my goal to become a Youth and Family Attorney. It was my belief that this was my purpose because of its personal connection to my own story. There was an attorney that helped me get emancipated as a minor, which allowed me to fund my way through college. She also offered me an internship within her office, which gave me insight into the influence and impact that individuals within her field could make on others. I believed that it would be my life's mission to advocate for children and families in the same way that she did for me. I did everything I could to align my actions in college with what I thought was my purpose. I engaged in volunteer work centered around youth and families, worked with at-risk students, engaged in policy and law internship for the State of Louisiana, as well as declared a major of Sociology with a concentration in Child & Youth Family Studies. I also took the LSAT exam with several schools showing some interest. Looks like I was doing a good job working towards my goal right?

One day while I researching and preparing to submit LSAT my profile to several schools, I received notification that I didn't meet the requirements for entrance into my top law school of choice. While they did offer an alternative admissions route, and I had several other great schools who did show interest, in that moment I experienced this internal feeling that I should not be

47

going into the field of law and instead began a career in education. For quite some time I never understood what caused me to make such a major shift after all of the hard work and planning I put into my life to lead to this moment. I didn't share emotion; I didn't even feel like I was letting go of my life's dream. I just simply shifted my thinking and said to myself, "ok, ill guess I start applying for teaching jobs, and plan for graduate school". I was able to secure my first full time teaching job in March, and was scheduled to graduate in May. I had also been accepted to graduate school and would be pursuing a Master's in Educational Leadership & Instruction. I was excited to walk across the stage with a degree, full-time job, and graduate schools plans already in place.

The funny thing about this story is that when I was searching for colleges after graduating high school, my older sister told me about a program at a large university that was specially geared towards males who expressed an interest in teaching. She informed me that she believed that as a man of color and with my story, I could thrive in education, and recommended that I consider. This program was offered at a top tier research institution (I didn't know the significance of that at the time), offering fully-funded scholarships, etc. I told her "NO," it was my plan to become an attorney.

> **Question:** How many people did God send in your life to say, "I think you should really think about......." Or "You have a personality for ...." "You're so good at...... I think you should purse......" Something happens to people when you do_____, have you ever thought about pursing it as a career, etc. etc. and your response was NO? I have found that the creator works so hard to get our attention to help us discover our purpose, but because of our selfish desires we disregard his nudging.

Why did I not want to be in education? It was not my personality. I am a quiet person and prefer to serve in more of a background focused space. While throughout my career, I have served as a teacher, administrator, and professor. Each of these types of roles consistently challenged my insecurities and put me in position to lead out front. I specially chose Child and Family Law as my career of interest because it not only connected to personal experiences in my life, to my knowledge at the time, courtrooms would probably be no more than three people besides the judge. I felt like could thrive in that space. I also liked the earning opportunities and created my own fantasies based on watching a lot of "Law & Order". My life's plan catered to my comfort zone and desires. We will dive deeper into this in another book, but it's important to know that your purpose is not about you. You must be prayerful and reflective. Asking the critical question, "why did I survive?" When I was born, what did the creator have in mind? How should I contribute to the earth? What generational curse I am called to break? When you discover the answers to those questions, it will more than likely make you uncomfortable, or challenge insecurities that may not have been addressed. Remember, it's not about you, it's about the message the creator wanted you to communicate to the earth.

Walking your purpose in life will be difficult. However, you should find comfort in knowing that you made this choice, and you will find all of your needs, wants, and some of your desires met. When I was considering being an attorney, I had no idea that there is a big focus on law and policy in the field of education.

Reflection

_____

_____

_____

_____

_____

_____

_____

_____

_____

_____

*People who live a life
of purpose have core beliefs and
values that
influence their decisions,
shape their day-to-day actions, and
determine their short- and long-
term priorities. They place
significant value on being a person
of high integrity and in earning the
trust and respect of others.
- Frank Sonnenberg*

Goal Worksheet

I believe that you should create goals in seven key areas of life. This worksheet will help you write your goals down and track them throughout the year. Goals without plans are merely dreams. Your goals should be measurable, unique to your personal journeys, time-sensitive, and serve as reminders of your game plan?

Goal	Category	Action Plan	Target Date
	Spiritual		
	Financial		
	Social		
	Physical		
	Intellectual		
	Career		
	Family		

Who's in your circle?

Authors Note: Oftentimes our bonds of friendship can be traced back to childhood or early adulthood when we were known as "the boys". Sometimes these relationships could have also been developed through "common dysfunction". One of the lessons I've learned throughout my journey is that your circle of friendships should complement your purpose. You should not be the smartest person within your peer group. Your circle should also evolve as you *grow*. How often do we maintain bonds with friends not because they "level us up," but because of common dysfunction? We know we need to broaden our peer group but this is who we know, we are comfortable with them, and they are a circle that never truly tells me the truth about me. We much rather maintain mental "prisons" then seek a different community to aid in our development. We fear rejection from our community if we decide to grow and the relationship must be re-defined. What if our failure to discover our purpose is tied to our inability to cultivate the right relationships? A great book to learn more about defining and realigning relationships is entitled *Relational Intelligence* by Dr. Dharius Daniels. *Iron sharpens iron, just as one man sharpens another. Proverbs 27:17 ESV*

Part I – My Current Circle

Name	When did you meet them?	What is their role?	Positive Impact on my life	Negative Impact on my life.

What Did You Learn from Part I?

_____

_____

_____

_____

_____

_____

_____

Suggested Types of Relationships

The Encourager:	• Someone that will pray with and for you, remind you of your Kingship, and give yourself grace.
The Truth-Teller:	• Someone focused on sheltering you with accountability, and honesty. I use the word "Shelter" because they do this privately. • They create a space where you can unplug and get honest feedback. This person does not gossip, and you will never have to worry about them informing others they had to correct you on something that you shared in confidence. • Their sole purpose is to help you become a better you and often challenge you to "level up." They also routinely inform you of "Blind-Spots."
The Wise One:	• Someone you can call and run ideas or challenges by. They have a solid spiritual foundation and the way they live their life will be evidence of their wisdom.

Other

Mentor	• Someone who is an expert in your field of aspiration. They can help you expand your thinking, give you access to opportunities, and encourage you to aim higher. Note: "They have been there and have done that."
Coach	• A person who is readily available to coach you through various problems within your career or personal life. They can provide you with clear actions steps and strategies.
Sponsor	• Someone that can sponsor you by speaking to your overall character.

Authors Note:

These types of relationships are merely recommendations for the main type of circle that all men should have around them. In a later book, I will be providing men of color with strategies focused on helping you develop and maintain these types of relationships.

Relationship Prayer

Dear Father-

Please help me to determine who I need to surround myself with to live out YOUR purpose for my life. Help me realize that relationships were your creation and that I was created for connection and not isolation. With your help, I will learn to continuously trust you and **NO LONGER** life my life through the lens of fear. Please give me clarity on what relationships that I may need to either remove or reassign in my life. Give me the GRACE to make these changes respectfully.

Give me the tools to stand firm in my decision and to not allow the negative reaction or projection of others to impact me.

I will **NO LONGER** allow others to negatively impact my potential or growth. I will view my relationships through a different lens and pray that you will send strong MEN to mentor, coach, encourage, and ultimately hold me accountable In Jesus name, Amen.

Living a Life of Purpose: **Resources & Ongoing Support**

30 Days of Affirmation

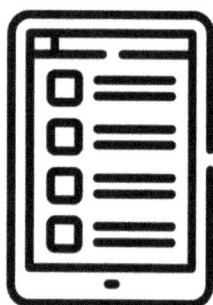

Author's Note: Affirmations are one of the most powerful and useful tools that we can apply to various aspects of our lives. Our words help shape our relationships, friendships, business, health, love, or daily moods. Affirmations can help you see your life's vision before it's manifested. Are you being kind to yourself with your words?

Day 1	• "I am confident, strong, and powerful."
Day 2	• "I bravely strive for what I want in my life."
Day 3	• "I am confident in social situations."
Day 4	• "I believe in myself."
Day 5	• "I always fight for myself and my beliefs."
Day 6	• "I boldly approach every challenge."

Day 7	• "I'm good with who I am, I'm proud of who I'm becoming."
Day 8	• "I'm done being used and taken advantage of."
Day 9	• "I won't give up when times get hard and things stop being easy."
Day 10	• "I have been given endless talents which I begin to utilize today."
Day 11	• "Impressing people isn't that important. I like who I am."
Day 12	• "I believe I can accomplish the goals I'm setting for myself. I'm being honest about what I want and I know why I need to accomplish these goals."
Day 13	• "I'm good with who I am, I'm proud of who I'm becoming."
Day 14	• "Currently, I'm not at the level I want to be but the more work I do, the better I'm going to get."
Day 15	• "I'm resilient. I can handle this."
Day 16	• "My confidence isn't built off compliments. It's built on mastery and competence."
Day 17	• "As I change my thoughts, the world around me changes."
Day 18	• "I am in the process of making positive changes in all areas of my life."
Day 19	• "My deepest desires are being fulfilled now."

Day 20	• "I value my worth. I am talented. I'm not going to sell myself short."
Day 21	• "I am guided in my every step by Spirit who leads me towards what I must know and do."
Day 22	• "I'll never give a person the power to use their words or actions to destroy my self-esteem."
Day 23	• "If you are using me or always putting me down, you don't have a place in my life."
Day 24	• "I define who I am. I decide what I do. My reputation is something I'll never fully have control over, but I can control how I live my life."
Day 25	• "I can only control what I do, I can't control what they think, say, or feel."
Day 26	• "I have to learn to speak up for myself. I can still be respectful but I have to let people know that they can't walk all over me."
Day 27	• "Regardless of the challenge, whatever is thrown in front of me is going to take care of it."
Day 28	• "No one can give me my purpose. It has to come from within."
Day 29	• "My journey of self-love isn't about me being selfish, it's about me becoming the best version of myself."

Day 30	• "I am worth something and I won't let anyone try to break me down."
(Source 61 Most Powerful Affirmations for Men- Shubham Shukla)	

You never know which experiences of life are going to be of value . . . You've got to leave yourself open to the hidden opportunities.
– Robin Roberts

First Read, Then Reflect, Next...How does this quote apply to my life?

_____

_____

_____

_____

_____

10 Scriptures About Purpose

But you are a chosen people, a royal priesthood, a holy nation, God's special possession, that you may declare the praises of him who called you out of darkness into his wonderful light. *-1 Peter 2:9*

For in him all things were created: things in heaven and on earth, visible and invisible, whether thrones or powers or rulers or authorities; all things have been created through him and for him. *-Colossian 1:16*

For I know the plans I have for you," declares the LORD, "plans to prosper you and not to harm you, plans to give you hope and a future.
-Jeremiah 29:11

I know that you can do all things; no purpose of yours can be thwarted. *-Job 42:2*

Many are the plans in a person's heart, but it is the LORD's purpose that prevails- *Proverbs 19:21*

For we are God's handiwork, created in Christ Jesus to do good works, which God prepared in advance for us to do. *- Ephesians 2:10*

And we know that in all things God works for the good of those who love him, who have been called according to his purpose. *- Romans 8:28*

Pray that you would bear fruit as you pursue the purpose God has appointed for you. "...I chose you and appointed you so that you might go and bear fruit—fruit that will last." *-John 15:16*

Each one should use whatever gift he has received to serve others, faithfully administering God's grace in its various forms. If anyone speaks, he should do it as one speaking the very words of God. If anyone serves, he should do it with the strength God provides, so that in all things God may be praised through Jesus Christ."- *1 Peter 4:10-11*

Be strong and courageous. Do not be terrified; do not be discouraged, for the LORD your God will be with you wherever you go."- Joshua 1:9

Source: Embracing Life: Pursuing Purpose

Prayers

Pray that you would surrender to the purpose that God has for you.
Pray that God would guide and direct you toward your purpose.
Pray that you would bear fruit as you pursue the purpose God has appointed for you.
Pray that God's will and purpose for you would be done
Pray that you would faithfully serve your purpose throughout your lifetime.
Thank God that He has empowered and equipped you with what you need to fulfill your purpose
Pray that you would confidently pursue the things God has uniquely crafted and called you to do.
Give thanks for how God has created you, blessed you, and for the things he is teaching you
Pray that God would use your circumstances, situations, gifts, and talents for his purpose and glory.

Source: Embracing Life: Pursuing Purpose

Scripture & Prayer Reflection

Scripture & Prayer Reflection

🏆 Celebrate #smallwins.

This section of the journal is focused on recording daily events. The idea here is that you want to write down whatever circumstance excites you, gives you the feeling that you've won.

_____
_____
_____
_____
_____
_____
_____
_____
_____
_____
_____
_____
_____
_____
_____
_____
_____
_____
_____
_____
_____
_____
_____
_____
_____
_____

✎ Daily Reflection

Daily Reflection

Daily Reflection

Daily Reflection

Daily Reflection

Daily Reflection

Daily Reflection

Daily Reflection

Daily Reflection

Daily Reflection

Daily Reflection

Daily Reflection

_____
_____
_____
_____
_____
_____
_____
_____
_____
_____
_____
_____
_____
_____
_____
_____
_____
_____
_____
_____
_____
_____
_____
_____

Daily Reflection

Daily Reflection

Daily Reflection

Daily Reflection

Daily Reflection

Daily Reflection

Daily Reflection

Daily Reflection

✎ Daily Reflection

Daily Reflection

Daily Reflection

Daily Reflection

Daily Reflection

Daily Reflection

_____

_____

_____

_____

_____

_____

_____

_____

_____

_____

_____

_____

_____

_____

_____

_____

_____

_____

_____

_____

_____

_____

_____

_____

_____

_____

_____

📝 Daily Reflection

Daily Reflection

Daily Reflection

Daily Reflection

Daily Reflection

Daily Reflection

Daily Reflection

Daily Reflection

Daily Reflection

Daily Reflection

www.ingramcontent.com/pod-product-compliance
Lightning Source LLC
Chambersburg PA
CBHW080920100426
42812CB00007B/2335